Money Savvy Ideas

JAYE THOMAS

Money Savvy Ideas
Copyright © 2020 by Jaye Thomas

All rights reserved. No part of this publication may be reproduced, distributed, or transmitted in any form or by any means, including photocopying, recording, or other electronic or mechanical methods, without the prior written permission of the author, except in the case of brief quotations embodied in critical reviews and certain other non-commercial uses permitted by copyright law.

Tellwell Talent
www.tellwell.ca

ISBN
978-0-2288-4211-8 (Hardcover)
978-0-2288-4210-1 (Paperback)
978-0-2288-4212-5 (eBook)

TABLE OF CONTENTS

Introduction v
My Story ix

Chapter 1 Benefits of Owning a Home 1
    Paying Off Your House 2
    Property 2
    Property Sharing 3

Chapter 2 Where to Start 5
    Substitution and Bulk Buying for Savings 5
    Saving Money on Products 6
    General Money-Saving Tips 7
    Clothes 8
    Food 9
    Health Products 11

Chapter 3 Doing Stuff around the House 13
    Cleaning 14
    Car 14
    Yard 16

Chapter 4 Online Deals, Vouchers and Discounts 18
    Store Loyalty Cards 19
    Added Bonuses 19

Chapter 5 Necessities and Bill Paying 21
    Get What You're Entitled to 22

    Household Bills including the Internet................................23
    Phone Bills...27
    Fuel..28
    Finance Companies 28
    Finance and Loans...30

Chapter 6   The Fun Stuff..31
    Shopping...31
    Travel...33
    Saving for Holidays..35
    The Fun Stuff..38
    Fitness..38

Chapter 7   The Way to Have Everything without Sacrifices ... 41

Chapter 8   Think outside the Box...44
    Make Money on the Side 45
    Using Your Skills 45
    Things That You No Longer Use..46
    Gift Ideas...48
    Hobbies 49

Conclusion: Positive Reinforcement 51
    Remain Motivated 51

INTRODUCTION

Wouldn't you love that sense of calm and satisfaction in your life, not having to stress about paying bills and not having to go without? Knowing that the money you earn is yours. Not having to stretch every cent of your hard-earned money to make ends meet. It really is the little things that do make a difference and that make life easier. To be able to still enjoy life, spend quality time doing things you love with family and friends. Set yourself up early while you have the money readily available to you so if and when times do get tough you can take a step back knowing that you've set yourself up in the best possible position already and you will still get by making minimum repayments until the opportunity arises again when you can increase payments to get ahead again. And you will know if these opportunities are the right ones to take. Listen to your intuition—feel your intuition and see what opportunities present themselves. I am here to share with you lots of different ideas, some of which you will think are brilliant and try yourself. Others you will think "what's this crazy woman talking about?" Pick and choose what works for you. There's always more than one way to skin a cat, as they say. I'm not one to dabble in shares, the stock market and the like, where you can lose a lot of money which otherwise could've been invested more wisely. Though the stock market may be something to look into in the future. On the other hand I have lots of friends who work on the theory that multiple properties negative geared is what works for them. Negative gearing is when you borrow money to invest usually to purchase properties and the income you receive from this investment ie. Rent, is less than your expenses (land rates, water rates, lawn maintenance) meaning their making a loss. One the property has increased value you sell the property and make a gain off the increased property value. You don't have to be as stingy in some areas or go without things you want or need. What works for one may not work for another. These are ideas to get you thinking outside the box. Make you aware of where your money is going. Where can you cut down your spending? What are you not willing to compromise on?

Goals are what keep us moving forward. Having something to achieve and work towards can be very uplifting when you can see that your hard work is beginning to pay off, when the results are starting to pop their head out of the sand to say "hi." The whole process and time it takes to save for your big goal. It may start as a hurdle or two, as frustrating as it may be. But if you know it's what you really want, then don't ever give up!

While I was typing up this book and discussing with friends and colleagues about what I'm writing, they all want to know what the book covers. Everyone wants to know what's in this book and how I managed to pay off my first house on my own in seven years on such a small income while still managing to travel the world and buy excess handbags and shoes. While trying to explain simply what's in the book, I would share some of my experiences to which I get a response of "so you purchase vouchers on Groupon (a website like marketplace that offers discount vouchers on activities, travel vouchers, goods and services)." Umm, in a nutshell—no! It's a much bigger picture than one solution. It's looking at every aspect of your life, what you want to get out of it. What you see as important to you, what you are happy to compromise on in an area to fulfil your desires in another.

What do you want to achieve? What are you goals? What do you want to save up for? It may be something big like a new car or a house, or it might be something small like a new watch or a dress for your birthday. Once you have an idea in mind, you can work out the amount of money that you want to need to save. Work out what you have left over in your pay cheque after putting money aside for bills and necessities and then put some aside each pay period to your desired item. Saving up for it and achieving your goal give you so much more appreciation towards it once you get it. That feeling that you earnt it yourself, you deserve it!

Planning is setting yourself in the right frame of mind of what goal you are working towards or what goal it is that you wish to achieve. What do you want to save up for? Do you want to go on an overseas holiday? Are you chasing that brand new car? How about a cute new pair of joggers? Set yourself a goal, give yourself something to strive towards, and get excited about what it is that you want to achieve and accomplish. Don't compare your goals to the goals of anyone else—not everyone wants to be a brain surgeon. We all have different talents and things that we can contribute. We weren't all put on this world to do the same thing. Otherwise, if we were all like-minded, creations like technology and electricity would never have come into play. We would not be here today to experience the joy and convenience of such items that we take for granted in our day-to-day living.

What do you want to save for: something small or something big? There is no right or wrong answer. This is brainstorming about what you want to achieve in life and what makes you happy. What makes you want to get out of bed in the morning with a bounce in your step and a smile on your face? Imagine the feeling of success once you've reached your goal. As you look back at your journey, the struggle makes the sense of accomplishment and fulfilment so much more satisfying knowing that you did this on your own. You achieved this goal, you made it happen! This feeling puts you on a path towards future and bigger successes.

What type of holiday do you want to go on? Where do you want to visit? Do have family relatives overseas that you've never met or friends that you've met that moved over that you want to go and visit? Is there an amazing overseas destination that you've seen on television or read about in a book and want to go visit and explore for yourself? Is your car always having dramas? Are you sick of renting and rental inspections and want your own place to call home without uplifting your life everything six months looking for another rental which that doesn't quite fit your criteria of close to the kids' school, the local gym or public transport for access to getting to work?

MY STORY

I don't believe in going without. Sure, some weeks I was a bit stingier than others, and some of the things I have done to save a few dollars would make you laugh. But laugh all you like. I may not be rich, I'm just an average girl, living an average life (I live and grew up in Australia, but have lived in most states New South Wales, Victoria, Western Australia and now currently residing in Queensland), trying to find my way in this big, changing world like the rest of us. Being rich shouldn't just be seen as being wealthy. Life is full of rich experiences. Yet I have managed to buy two properties on my own, while still travelling to all corners of the world and experiencing everything from musicals and concerts to shopping and buying my favourite fitness tights and joggers.

In the days back in the early nineties and 2000 it used to be frowned upon to be a savvy shopper. But in today's era, you're in luck, as savvy shopping has now become trendy, fashionable, the in thing. Everyone wants to know how to save a dollar. Everyone wants to know the secret to living a more comfortable life while still having money left over to do whatever they please.

In order to save money in some cases, you may need to follow up what you're entitled to more than once unfortunately. Does it get you out of your comfort zone? Yes. Does making that phone call make you feel awkward? Yes. Do you want your money back? I know I do. Even in the past couple of weeks I've dealt with big companies and little companies. Be polite. Despite being in the right, you still do want your refund, and you deserve what you're entitled to. You don't want someone holding a grudge and holding back just to make your life difficult.

My dream was to pay off my house in five years. Okay, so it took me seven-and-a-half years, but still it's an achievement. I did buy at a good time, mind you that was pure luck, but I was around when interest rates were over 8% not today's fixed term of 4%! I bought while still managing along the way to have it all—from overseas holidays (once a year), a brand new car (my pride and joy Mazda3), the latest fashions (or so I thought they were) and parties on a regular basis. I still managed to do it on a single income. I wasn't on a fortune either, I didn't get any help or handouts from anyone along the way. I just picked up ideas, set a budget of what I had to work with and you find a way to make it work. It's just little things along the way from only going for a daytrip when you have a voucher to the animal park at a discounted rate, saving $5 on petrol each week due to buying on the cheap end of the petrol cycle, to only buying you're favourite green juice at the supermarket when it's on sale, set a goal, the amount you're allowed to spend per fortnight and there are ways to live within this amount. Whatever goal you are saving towards, the new car, that new piece of gym equipment so you train at home without paying for gym fees, whatever you wish to achieve put your mind to it and you can achieve this goal if this is what you really want!

Money-saving ideas can become stagnant, though that's all part of the process. If one thing isn't working then try something else. Keep trying until you find what works for you. I've recently just purchased my second home, and yes, it has been frustrating to say the least. Starting off with a $450,000-home loan, I found out that I was going to have to spend my savings to pay the initial down payment of 20%. Yes, that's what savings are for, but in the meantime I was making money off that money just sitting there. The bank took too long to approve the loan so I went ahead anyway. The good news today is that from a $404,000 loan, I have now saved myself another $10,000, dropping my loan further again to under $400,000.

Currently, I'm sorting out re-financing for my rental property. I now own two houses before the age of 35, and I did this all on my own. Yes, there have been times of struggle, especially the frustration you go through with the banks. It is so much easier and less hassle to get a broker involved to help deal with the banks for you.

Right now that is the position I have found myself in again. Think back to when you started your previous jobs. You weren't the boss straight away or running the show. We all have to start somewhere and sometimes that means taking a step back. Opportunities will arise. You just need to be there, stay upbeat and positive, and reflect if need be on your previous progression and how you got where you are today. You'll be surprised what comes to light and what you can use to your advantage to help you get ahead in your particular field.

Once you notice the change, see the difference and notice the results, other ideas will start flowing and come to light. You'll be inspired and creative in finding other avenues, means of saving or creating extra income that you least expected.

CHAPTER ONE

BENEFITS OF OWNING A HOME

Here's me, currently planning my trips away for the year, snowfields here I come. If my house wasn't paid off (my initial home was paid off so this became my rental property -which paid for itself due to the tenants regular rent repayments-the money on the house I owned, I paid off the second house with, which is now the house I live in. Therefore the only mortgage I was paying was the original owned property that the tenants were living in and they covered the expenses with their rent payment. I wouldn't be able to partake in random, spur-of-the-moment decisions without having to save up for a trip away. If you are paying off a house, that shouldn't stop you from having a life and enjoying the finer things it has to offer. We don't just live to work; we don't just work to pay the bills. What a boring life that would be! It would so very monotonous that you'd end up with no drive or passion to actually get out of bed in the morning and actually get out there. You need that work-life balance. As much as the next person I'd give anything to quit work and just travel, which I was actually planning a couple of years back until I realised I could have the best of both worlds. But eventually the money would run out. If you aren't working, you don't enjoy the downtime as much. While working hard, you definitely appreciate your hard-earned money and it gives you something to work towards. You can see the results of where all your hard work, time and effort have gone.

Paying Off Your House

Some people believe that whatever money can you save, you should be putting it all into your mortgage repayments. Yes and no. Here's the way I did it on my first property: I paid double what the loan repayments were onto the mortgage. I am using a similar approach on my second property, as it worked really well for me the first time around.

Any extra money I saved in other areas of my life was a bonus to me. For example, I save money by: lowering my electricity bill; buying fuel on sale and using a voucher; and substituting higher priced food with similar products for a cheaper price. Whenever I found extra money, I used that to treat myself to a pretty new perfume or moisturiser, or that notepad I've had my eye on. You've got to treat yourself. Otherwise you will lose the excitement and drive to save money. You'll feel like you're saving for nothing or have nothing to show for it. Give yourself those rewards, and acknowledge how far you've come and how well you're doing. You need to have small things in the distance to reward yourself.

Property

One of my friends recently purchased a property. He was so insistent that that's what he had to do. I remember that feeling, being lost, not knowing if you're headed in the right direction, but feeling that you can't sit still any longer any more. Talk to someone to get it off your chest, because talking it out loud can help you process what you're thinking a lot clearer. Or write it down. Make a list of the pros and cons, and see which way you're leaning more towards. Listen to other people's advice, especially those who have been through similar situations, as they may bring to light the answers that you need. There's no point in spending all this money on an overpriced property that brings you no returns as an investment or loses value in the long run due to purchasing at the wrong time of the market. Yes, there is a right and wrong market time to purchase, so use it to your benefit and get that amazing house in that awesome area for the best price. You'd be surprised what opportunities present themselves in many forms for return on investment, such as the house that has an urgent sale due to family reasons that has been reduced in price.

Property Sharing

It's not about where in the country is the best location to buy a property or what type of property will have the best resale value or chance at getting rented out quickly to bring in an income to cover the cost of another mortgage repayment. Though for people interested in the property market for investment purposes, this maybe an avenue for you.

Just because your house has a spare room, doesn't mean that you have to rent it out to someone. Sure, that may be nice and help accelerate the process of paying off your house quicker. But some people have a family or young children, or they just might like their own company and not want to deal with squabbles with lazy housemates over whose turn it is to take out the trash or who drank the last of "my" milk in the refrigerator. Sometimes those extra hassles are not worth saving money over.

Other times having the comfort that you've someone to talk to after a hard day at work can be just what you need, or having that security in knowing that you've someone living there when you're not home. These are some of the things that you have to weigh for yourself as to which option may help your current financial situation. Just make sure they pay the rent and share the bills!

Don't get me wrong as I have had housemates and they're not all horror stories. Sometimes people clash and have a different way of going about things. Providing there's no disrespect for other people's privacy and personal belongings, we are all adults and should be able to talk about what's bugging us and getting on our nerves with those around us—in a polite manner, of course.

CHAPTER TWO

WHERE TO START

Substitution and Bulk Buying for Savings

Sometimes a more expensive product doesn't necessarily mean that it is a better-quality product or that it is better value for the money. You can pay more for something and it can last much longer, same as with home renovations and car services. Ask around and ask your friends what companies work well for them or have received really good service from. You can also look up the company or product online where they usually have customer comments and feedback on previous service. That's how I solve a lot of my decision-making dilemmas. Some people use the "three quote rule," meaning that they ring and enquire to receive three quotes and see which one offers the best value for money or deal for the service they require.

There are always generic products available on the market, which are most often cheaper. If you're like me, you won't compromise on quality as it will cost you more in the long run. What stores do bulk purchasing? Online ordering these days is usually always available at a fraction of the cost and sometimes even quicker delivery than waiting for the store to order the product in for you. Alternatively, you can always wait for sales or you can compromise in another area of your spending that you are willing to be more lenient on. The big question with any purchase is "do you really need it?" Or are you like me and have a container full of lip glosses but still really need to have that glossy one on special at the checkout?

Marketing ploys are everywhere you look these days. Everyone is out to try and get your money to one degree or another. We all need to make a living. Never, ever go food shopping on an empty stomach. I'm sure you've heard the saying before if you haven't already experienced it yourself. It's like this uncontrollable urge or force that takes over from within. Memories come flooding back of the last time you tasted or experienced the melt of the chocolate chip cookie in your mouth. If you're like me, you say "just one more" and you don't stop at one. Suddenly half the box is gone just on the drive home alone, and you wonder "why did I just do that? I wasn't even hungry."

I don't like the ravishing, uncontrollable anger that erupts when you have to have something. There's no turning back when you get to that point. That savage beast within needs to be fed to feel calm and satiate the desire.

Saving Money on Products

There are many ways you can save money—you just need to look and think outside the box. Focus on what's important to you or what you can go without or are willing to sacrifice to achieve what your passion is, what your heart desires in life are. Not everyone wants to use the same products. I will not compromise on quality on hair-care products, but I know a girl I work with is just like that but with loaves of bread. But I would be willing to save a few dollars on bread if that meant I was using that money towards spending money for an overseas trip.

Some generic products aren't as similar to your favourite product. If you're not willing to substitute for a similar product as it doesn't fit your expectations, then don't, as ultimately the final decision always lies with you. This is about making it as easy as possible for you and of course a bit of fun and imagination in saving money in other areas in your life so you can enjoy what is more important to you and get ahead, creating a more carefree future to enjoy.

Chemists (as they are known in Australia otherwise sometimes called pharmacists in other countries) are a big one for generic brands. When you go to the chemist for everyday subscriptions, they usually offer the chemists' own brand or ask if you're happy to purchase the cheaper, generic version of the same product, which also contains the same ingredients.

General Money-Saving Tips

With saving money, remember that every little bit helps, from putting extra on the mortgage than the minimum payment to paying fortnightly rather than monthly (as it equals out over a year that there is an extra payment paid). I know interest-only loans don't allow you to have that option, but you could always put extra aside into a separate account to be transferred at a later stage back onto the mortgage once the interest-only loan has finished. For example, if your fortnightly repayments are $700, even adding an extra $50 will reduce your home loan over the years.

Even as a kid, I used to budget even the smallest amount of money. I would divide up my $2.50 pocket money into separate containers: one for stamps, one for gifts, one for me.

Even today that's how I still manage my money to a degree: pay everything else first before paying myself. You will hear a lot of people tell you to pay yourself first. But sometimes there are fortnights when an unexpected bill may pop up or the bill may be larger than you anticipated. The bills still need to be paid. This is when calculating your yearly bills ahead of time comes in handy. Take this as an opportunity to clear out a closet to make some extra dollars online by selling items you no longer need. Or carpool to work or use up leftovers in the cupboard for meals to help get you through until the next pay period. There are always other ways to bring an abundance of money to you to help get you through lean times.

When it comes to getting to and from work, if it's not within walking distance and you're feeling fit, you could ride a bike to work, increasing your fitness at the same time as saving money on fuel and saving the environment. Or you could ask around at work to find someone to carpool with and take turns driving to work. Or you could carpool with friends in the local area. This in turn will save you mileage on your car and also give you a travel buddy.

Sometimes people refuse to scrimp on things like toilet paper, and that's okay. Find something else that you can compromise on price without compromising quality, like utilising a cheaper brand of chux (Australian version of re-useable cloths for cleaning and wiping surfaces) or tissues. Alternatively, substitute with something else, or read this week's store sales catalogue to help make a difference by saving some extra money from your shopping bill.

Clothes

I like to save, doesn't everyone? But I also like to dress fashionably and nicely without the added cost and expense. You don't have to wear the most expensive outfit, there are a lot of nice, fashionable clothing stores always with a sale or bargain to get you in the door, to get your business. Some stores sell generic lookalike items or a cheaper brand, just as good a quality without the price tag. Just because it's on special does not mean that it's a good deal or that it's the right deal for you. Basic essentials and accessories come in handy to jazz up an outfit or turn a summer dress into a winter piece. Think outside the box, be creative, look at magazines or store displays for inspiration and ideas of how to use the pieces you currently have in your wardrobe.

Clothing outlets are very popular and fashionable these days. There are outlet malls trying to sell off excess stock, last season's outfits, and faulty or dirty items, which are easy to fix with a needle and thread or a wash in the machine at home. They offer deals if you buy two items and then get the third free. Take a friend—that's the best way if you can't find enough items to fulfil a deal. Sometimes it's better to pass up an offer than only get half of the deal.

Food

There is so much food wastage these days, whether it's in the working environment or at home because too much food has been purchased and is not being utilised prior to going out of date or rotting before you use it. Food items can be purchased in smaller quantities, which will save you money, prevent waste and not fill up the landfill. Your food will stay fresh as it hasn't been sitting in the fridge for weeks. You will get used to knowing how much of which products you go through, what you always run out of or what you never actually finish using up. You could always make note of what products are expiring within the next couple of days to ensure you make a meal involving that item, which saves money and also adds variety to your meals. In turn, you learn to not overbuy some products over others.

These days shops have extended hours, so there isn't that need to rush in and stock up. Buy only what you need for a few days rather than a week of fruit and vegetables which will only wither away and be unusable except to feed the bunny rabbits.

I do all my bulk fruit and vegetable shopping at a warehouse outlet. Plus it's always a good feeling to give back to the farmers by purchasing from those stalls on the side of the road or many farmers markets. A lot of the time their products are just as cheap or even cheaper than buying at a supermarket and they are usually fresher and taste better than from commercial supermarkets. It's cheaper to buy in bulk, most stores these days do loyalty cards where you earn points for each dollar you spend in the store. Once you earn so many points you receive vouchers, especially when you're already buying the product.

I regularly check the catalogues for the supermarkets that come in the mail so way I'm aware of the cost of regular purchased items. Why pay the full amount when you don't have to? There's a big enough market out there that you can get the best possible deal within a few stores.

Use those vouchers and collect those points if it's local and where you would normally shop. Get those benefits and entitlements that come your way. There is nothing more fulfilling than receiving something for free for doing what you normally would do.

There is nothing worse than overbuying perishables and they go out of date before you use them. A really good idea with bulk meat is to plastic wrap it in portion sizes to freeze, making it easier to defrost and having less waste. Cooking up bulk stews and soups and freezing for a meal on the run save time in this busy world that we live in.

When you have takeaway meals from restaurants like Chinese, keep the containers, wash them out and reuse them. They can be used for taking snacks to work or saving leftovers from dinner the night before. It saves money on plastic wrap by using a sealed container and it's also easier for transporting to and from work or to school for the kids.

Even the cost of bottled water can become quite expensive. There are cheaper alternatives. If you don't like the taste of filling up with tap water, you can get bottles with filters attached to them, or alternatively you can purchase filters to attach to your tap. If you want to have more money for yourself and whatever it is that you're saving up for, you need to make comprises, but how extreme you wish to go is your choice entirely.

We all do like some things that aren't always that good for us, like the occasional sweet treat. Sad but true, I'm a sucker for sweet products, like I'm sure many of you have your own sweet indulgences that you cave in for. A lot of stores have end-of-the-day specials as items are going out of date or bakery items won't be as fresh the next day for customers. Or they have a rummage bin where damaged items can be purchased for a much cheaper price due to a dent in the box or some imperfection that isn't fit for selling at the full price.

Health Products

Health supplements and foods for athletes, such as pre-workout and protein energy bars, are a massive market these days. Those companies focusing of fitness and health make a fortune. I personally have tried many supplements and suppressants myself. Ask around and see which products friends use or what they recommend. Try or taste a product they use prior to buying. There is no point spending all this money on a product that you aren't going to get the benefits from or use due to the taste not agreeing with you.

CHAPTER THREE

DOING STUFF AROUND THE HOUSE

I'm a big believer in using things up until the very end, from getting that very last fingernail scrape of moisturiser out of the tub to that last squirt of the rolled-up toothpaste tube and even to the point of cutting open lip glosses and scooping out the remainder. You'd be amazed at how many extra days of use you can get out of an item.

It's not just everyday items that you can save money on and give an extended life. You can also look around the house for things that are long overdue that need doing, such as decluttering wardrobes to be or doing general maintenance jobs. Sure, having the convenience to pay someone to come and tidy up the house or yard is stress-free, but imagine the feeling of accomplishment to know that you have achieved it all on your own.

Painting the house is a big one as it costs thousands of dollars to hire someone to paint your house. Just because a professional has done the job that doesn't mean that you will be happy with the end result either (though you would want them to do a decent job since you're paying them you're hard earned money) and especially spending that kind of money you want to know that it's a reputable company and money well spent.

In the technology world of today, you can look up how-to guides on YouTube, Google and the likes or anything and everything your heart desires. Even the girliest girls like myself can learn how to mow the lawn, change a washer in the shower (that's not to say there hasn't been the accidental incident of almost flooding one's bedroom due to forgetting to isolate the water mains), change a lightbulb and whatever else the mind can imagine or wish to learn. You no longer have to rely on a man about the house for everything.

Cleaning

Look inside those cupboards and pantries. Everywhere from the kitchen to the bathroom and the bedroom, we all have things that we never use, such as those sheets sitting at the back of the cupboard that we don't like the material of. We have kitchen appliances still in the box given as a gift from last Christmas or those worn non-stick-coated frypans that are beyond usable. Once you start clearing out the clutter, you'll be amazed what you find that you no longer use or need and can be sold online or donated towards a charity (if in good enough working order).

Car

What works for one person may not necessarily work for another, like the time my friend told me to see a financial advisor. I am a very stubborn person as it is, without someone to try and tell me how to do things. I was told to sell my car and a buy a brand new car. To me at that time of my life, it was a complete waste of time and money when my focus was on paying off the mortgage. His belief was that to make money, you had to spend money. Yes and no. I was paying quite a lot in car services and repairs, meaning in the long run a new car would cut my car service costs by a half to a third. To me that wasn't making leeway in the right direction of where I wanted to be headed especially when you look at how much money you would be spending in one lump sum to buy the car in the beginning.

This is not to disregard all financial advice. I myself have made mistakes rushing into things, without looking at the bigger picture or consequence of my choices not working out as I thought they would. Everyone has their own ideas. If a financial advisor won't listen to you and only want to do things their way, that is not going to benefit you in the long run. There are always other financial advisors you can see or get advice from friends who have been through a similar situation and can guide you on the right path. Ultimately the end decision lies in your hands. Remember though if you want to get ahead, sometimes drastic measures need to be taken to see a difference.

A couple of years later, I did buy a brand new car, while still paying off the mortgage—it can be done. As the old saying goes, if someone tells you to jump off a bridge, would you? This may not be as serious question as it may seem. What do you want to achieve? Remember the old saying of "where do you see yourself in five years?" It's a question a lot of us don't really think about a lot of the time. We just go through life, day after day, getting by, mindlessly plodding along … and then what?

Sometimes it is worth spending a little bit of money to give yourself some free time. I used to wash my own car. By the time you set up all the equipment (that's if you're not living in an area where there are water restrictions or no outside access to wash your car like living in apartments) and dry it quickly enough before the sun streaks it, it may not be worth all the hassle, especially when you can go through the local car wash and get two car washes for $20, with a 60-day expiry use. Not to mention they have awesome high-pressure vacuum cleaners that you don't have to pack up after use for only a dollar a minute—spare change. Then you drive off about your own day-to-day business—now that's what I call no hassle.

You can wash your car at home and actually do a better job than taking it to the car wash where they charge you about $20 and it looks like it wasn't even washed. What a total waste of money! Just by buying a bucket, sponge, polish and chamois cloth, you make your money back after the first wash. This applies if you don't live in an area where there are water restrictions or you're simply not allowed to wash your car in your complex. If this is the case and you can't drop by your friends place and get them to wash it for you, car companies do entice return service for washes after so many visits like your coffee shop does.

Yard

We all have house maintenance that we want to get done or fix-up projects around the house. There are things you can do around the yard without paying for handy workers. People talk about having a barbecue and inviting friends over to help with the weeding, but unfortunately I've never been able to get anyone interested, no matter how much beer is involved. I think it might also be because everyone else has so many things going on in their own lives that they also need to sort out and get on top of.

A big house maintenance job is my yard. After weeding for hours and hours, it seemed like I was never getting anywhere while my next door neighbour's yard looked immaculate. I bumped into their lawn mower man (nothing like going straight to the source) and got him to spray my yard and it never looked better and came out amazing. This was better than going through a phone book when you haven't been able to see the quality of a company's work or service.

It can cost a lot of money to get your lawn mowed and your gardens maintained and weeded. But just a little work every couple of weeks is enough to keep it looking nice and presentable. Okay, so I'm not the best yard worker or that thrilled with looking after gardens. It's definitely not my cup of tea, but I get by. If it really is too much, you can always pay for a one-off massive cleanup and then maintain it from there, making it easier on your time and money and efficiency wise as well. I have to admit I've done that once or twice, and it's a really good idea especially at the beginning of the season. Get it out of the way early so you can enjoy the nice weather entertaining guests or playing sports in the yard with the kids.

If I need to hire someone or am looking for advice, I find that putting it up on Facebook or other social media gets a decent response from people who have firsthand experience. People love giving advice for whom they recommend or what services worked for them. In these days of a self-employed environment, someone always knows someone with a business.

CHAPTER FOUR

ONLINE DEALS, VOUCHERS AND DISCOUNTS

Many companies these days offer value deals from combining multiple purchases or package deals at a discounted price for a limited time. Some of these companies include Living Social, Groupon, Shopping Square, Catch of the day, Booking.com, Agoda, OpenRoomz. There is an online company or app for anything and everything these days! I have booked quite a few trips myself through these companies and received further discounts for my next trip for becoming a frequent user.

Just because its online doesn't always mean that it's a good deal though. Make sure you always read the fine print and aren't getting yourself committed to something else attached to what you thought you were purchasing. I once won a bid for a singlet on eBay that was way too small for me. I was so excited for the product that I didn't pay any attention to the size that I was bidding on or the fact that nobody was bidding against me. Luckily, I was a regular buyer with this company and they allowed me to swap it for another item. Make sure you use only reliable websites as you still hear of people these days getting hacked or products not being delivered for whatever reason. There's nothing worse than buying yourself an amazing trip overseas to find out you can't get time off over the period that you're only allowed to travel in or the hotel is actually all booked for the dates that you're there.

These days you can look up almost anything online and get an idea of how much a product is worth. You can also find the best deal and take it into a store and see if they can work out a deal for you to get your business. There are three advantages of buying in-store rather than online. If you have any problems after you've taken the product home, you have a qualified sales person to go to for advice. You're not paying unnecessary postage to return the item if repairs are required, and you're also keeping people in jobs.

Store Loyalty Cards

Sometimes you can be inundated with too many email vouchers and deals. You don't need to sign up for everything to get yourself a good deal. If anything, you'll probably end up wanting to buy everything or have a wallet full of card that you never use.

You don't need to have a card for every store. But if you do have a favourite store or somewhere that you regularly shop, the cards definitely have their advantages, especially when you're going to purchase the item anyway, like fuel and food. All the points accrue and you can get vouchers too.

Added Bonuses

At the supermarket there are so many products available to purchase that one can easily be inundated with information overload or indecisiveness due to confusion of which product to choose. One factor that helps me in deciding what product I purchase is if there's any special promotions that will benefit me. Recently I got a free magazine subscription just for purchasing three dishwashing liquids. It was something that I needed to buy anyway, with the added freebie being a bonus. Some cheaper alternatives are just as good as the real thing.

CHAPTER FIVE

NECESSITIES AND BILL PAYING

When going through your pay cheque, first put aside money for bills that must be paid. You don't want to go without electricity and not be able to enjoy your favourite show on a rainy evening on a cold winter's night while attempting to cook up a pot of soup for the week's lunch meals. Not paying bills on time leads to overdue fees, money that could be put towards next month's bills.

Here's a little trick that I like to use. My credit card—like all—has an end month date (not necessarily the end of the month though) before it resets for the next month statement. If you time it right, you can pay for your bills as the statement has reset, giving yourself a further two months opposed to one month to pay the bill.

Some people believe once you're behind, you'll always be behind. As a homeowner, if you chart your bills, you will know what months you have more bills to pay than others. Rather than dipping into that savings account, increasing your home loan repayments or put a small portion away each pay period so that when the credit card bill is due you have the money to pay it. Yes, some people say you should save 10% or some amount of your wage and you should have so many thousands of dollars stashed away in another account. But today with low wages and ever-increasing utility bills, that may not always be an option. When there are alternatives that do the same thing why not give it a go? I do hear some people say, "But if I have a credit card, I'll use it." But that's like having cookies in the cupboard and wanting to eat the entire packet. Sometimes restraint may need to be enforced. Alternatively give your credit card to someone trusted like a family member until these situations arise when you really do need it to help out financially.

Get What You're Entitled to

Check your bank statements. You may be surprised at what you find. I previously cancelled a course, got my deposit refunded yet they continued to take fortnightly payments out of my account. If I wasn't so efficient at tracking my accounts, despite not even having purchased anything recently, I may not have even noticed these charges. Thankfully these days, technologies and apps make it very easy and quick to stay on top of your bank balances and transactions. The sooner you get onto it, the better, especially when they take so long to refund money. But when they take it, it's instant. For refunds, sometimes you have to be prepared to wait and always make sure that it does go back into your account.

Money can be lost simply by not chasing up or checking statements and being charged incorrectly. I found out I've been paying double house insurance for most of the year. Don't settle on the fact that you've made a mistake. Instead, ring and enquire, as I did and I ended up being able to get the entire amount refunded to me. Having a history with a company for a long period of time also gives you the extra advantage of being a regular customer. For extra charges to your credit card, dispute them and don't pay for something that you haven't purchased. Companies can make mistakes too so always check your statements. There's no point losing your hard-earned money to other people or companies. You've worked hard for that, and mistakes shouldn't happen, but unfortunately sometimes they do. You shouldn't walk around with your head in the sand; if there's something you can do about it, then do it. This is your money we're talking about. Make it work for you. You have worked hard for it.

Household Bills including the Internet

To manage bills, I calculate how many times per year that bill is paid, for example, monthly, every three months or yearly. If it's bills like Motor vehicle registration and insurance, allow for increase in yearly premiums. Write down all the bills you pay, including mobile phone, house phone, private health, water, land rates (charged by local government on property you own and include charges for waste management, city transport improvement and recreational space fees), water rates, insurance, and roadside assistance. Once they are all listed, tally up your yearly cost. Divide by 26 fortnights per year and that will give you the total amount you need to put aside to cover all your bills. Always round up, for example, if it's $285, make it $300. It's always better to have excess than to run short, especially when things seem to be constantly increasing in cost these days.

Utility and insurance companies offer discounts if you pay yearly rather than monthly. For me paying my rates yearly was saving me an extra $400 a year that could be spent elsewhere. Now that does make a difference.

I'm lucky in the fact that my house has evaporative air conditioning, because refrigerate uses too much power. There are other methods to keep cool in summer and warm in winter, especially if you want to see those extra dollars to be utilised elsewhere. Make that difference!! Save up for that holiday. Pay for that house. It's those small changes you make that do make the difference.

I'll let you in on a secret: credit card and finance companies aren't necessarily bad if you use them to your advantage, plus it will give you a good credit rating. Some people are dead set against using credit cards, but that's how I got where I am today. I used them to my advantage. If you know something works for you, don't listen to what anyone else has to say, within reason of course. I am a very stubborn person, I like doing things my own way and I adapt things to what suits me and works well for my situation.

Here's how I have used them to my advantage over the years and will continue to use them. I don't believe in spending my own money when it can be sitting in the bank earning interest when I can use someone else's—like financial companies. I have a credit card that has no annual fee. Always pay your bills prior to their due date so you don't get stung with late fees, and then you won't have a problem.

Large bills like land rates (in Australia rates are taxes the local government charge on properties in their area), water rates and house insurance don't usually give you more than a couple of weeks to pay over a thousand dollars, which isn't even a pay packet for most people. To bide yourself time, pay your bill using your credit card if you don't have money already saved up. Like I previously mentioned, if you get to know your credit card you will notice what is the cut-off date for that month. Sometimes I get lucky and get a whole two months to pay back a bill. When that happens, you don't wait two months to pay the credit card. You pay fortnightly a quarter of the bill to ensure you still pay the credit card prior to the due date. I still use this method today, despite owning my own home.

Some people frown upon the use of credit cards, but if you go about it the right way, you can turn it to your advantage. There are cards that have zero annual fees if you're not one to spend up to make use of frequent flyer points or the like. I found if you time it right, you can give yourself an extra month to pay your bill. Only go this way if you pay the bill on time. You won't get any benefits if you end up paying interest to the credit companies. The money is better in your bank account accruing interest, even if it's only $15. It's better in your pocket than theirs. It's a great way to pay your bills if you're strapped for cash that month.

Imagine how you feel once you have achieved your goal. Those small sacrifices that you've made along the way will feel like nothing. They're not even sacrifices—look at it as substitution, using different ideas, trying different things. The more ideas you branch out into, the more ideas will come to you that you will get excited about and want to try out.

A lot of money can be saved by going through your bills to make sure you're getting the best deal possible and not getting charged late fees. Every day, watch your utilities usage in and around the house to help reduce your monthly bills. I've always kept my electricity bill low by turning off devices not being used. As the old saying goes, if it's still turned on at the wall, it's still using electricity. Items like the washing machine, the dryer, microwave and television aren't used all the time and therefore don't need to be left on. You should be at work during the day. At the beginning, you may think it's a hassle turning the switches off. But like anything, it's a habit and once you do it for a while, it will become second nature and part of your routine.

Clothes dryers use a lot of power. If the weather's nice, use that extra 10 minutes to hang your load on the line. It makes your clothes last longer, with less chance of your clothes shrinking. If the weather doesn't permit, hang your clothes on an indoor clothesline or clothes rack.

Once you see a difference in your electricity bill and how much money that you have saved, that alone will give you inspiration. You will become motivated to look for other money-saving avenues.

One thing that can really make a big difference is what companies you currently go through for insurance. You can get deals if you combine them all in one company. Private health is a big expense today, especially at tax time, when there's nothing worse than getting charged the same as though you were receiving private health insurance but not actually receiving any benefits. Companies do packages where you only pay for what you use. There's no need paying for pregnancy health services if that's not something that you're planning in the near future.

Just because it was a good rate when you signed up to that health insurance, house insurance, home loan, or whatever it maybe, that doesn't mean that its competitive in today's market. Ask around, as some friends may be comfortable talking about what companies they've had a great experience with. There are even online comparison sites that do the looking for you. Staying online half an hour to get one quote after another may not be your cup of tea. Markets change, so take advantage of it and you might be surprised what savings you can excite yourself with. That's it, be excited! It is fun to find ways to save money without actually selling your favourite handbag for one tenth of the cost online or cutting back on those delicious chocolate chip cookies that taste so much better in your favourite brand.

Phone Bills

There are so many phone plans on offer—different caps, bundles and deals, what do you choose? What is going to work for you? What are you going to get benefits from? At one stage one company was giving me a free phone every two years and my plan was unlimited, never going over my limit or getting overcharged for my plan. Sometimes I didn't like the free phone they were offering, but I accepted it due it being a bonus as a regular customer and sold it to friends or second-hand shops.

Nowadays, that doesn't suit me, so I switched to a cap. I started off on a cheap one, but found I was reloading more often, so upping the plan gave me more value for my money. Caps are good for people who travel a lot and don't use international roaming. You don't want to be paying for a service you're not using or getting the benefits from.

Phone companies provide deals that include so many calls and texts for one price. Better value is to get a prepaid plan. Then if you go over your cap, you run out of credit rather than adding onto your total. Alternatively if you love the latest gadgets and keeping up with technology so your device works more efficiently, then get a plan in which you get a free phone at the same time.

At the same time, plans do outlive themselves. Prior to coming to the end of your contract you should have an idea of what you need out of your phone plan. Is it more data or outgoing calls? Going off your previous plan, what did you always run out of? You don't always have to stick with the same company, unless of course you're in mining and they only get reception from one server. Weigh up whether the extra you've previous been spending on your bill is worth it or whether cutting your plan short and going elsewhere might actually save you more money in the long run.

Here's another trick to extend your phone data. When I am low on credit towards the end of the month, I use my iPad or home wireless, which has a larger data plan. A lot of public places, from coffee shops to fast-food outlets, offer free Wi-Fi so use that time to do your phone updates and downloads.

Fuel

In some states there's certain days during the week that are cheaper to buy fuel than others. They have fuel patterns or you usually will notice, simply from driving around, which stores in which areas trend to advertise cheaper prices a majority of the time. Every little bit helps these days. Most supermarkets give you fuel vouchers when you spend a certain amount of money. If you're already buying the products, then it's an added bonus as you are getting something for what you were buying.

It's amazing how much fuel prices can change from store to store. I'm not one to drive miles out of the way for fuel, as you don't really get your money's worth if you spend all your fuel looking for a bargain. Do your research first. They even have online websites where you can request daily emails to be sent to you on the prices at local stores near you. You'll find they usually have a day during the week that's the cheapest—fill up on those days.

Finance Companies

There are several finance companies around. Check what the monthly account-keeping fees are. Usually they're the same as the bank charges you for your account. Also check what the fee is for the initial set up. Myself I found it easier and cheaper to keep an account open rather than closing and reopening as I decide to purchase a high-cost product like furniture for my home.

All the furniture in my house has been bought this way, by using finance companies on interest free repayments. Why spend your hard earned money when you can keep it aside for a rainy day or when you really need it. I'm not a fan of the layby (you pay by instalments and the goods are held by the retailer until you pay off the balance) where you wait for months to receive your product to be able to use it and by that stage there's something better on the market or your product has now become superseded.

The trick I use is to only make a purchase when a store has a promotion, for example, the most recent one that I've taken advantage of is a 50-month interest-free loan. I bought a new outdoor lounge, a new oven and a new house phone, which I thought I'd throw in since my old one was sounding echoey and no one could hear me properly on the other end and never wanted to talk anyway. My repayments are only $50 a fortnight and I got them to price match the items from another store because I looked around and did my research.

People are always looking at upgrading their furniture and household goods for something more updated or suited to their expanding family or they move houses and need to change their furniture to fit into the style and measurements of the new place. Don't say that you don't have the time to look around to compare prices to save yourself a few dollars. That's what the internet is there for. You do the research. No one else is going to do the research for you. You want to save money, so make the time and put in the effort to make it happen.

Once you start noticing the differences, such as you have new furniture at a small price or you have extra money from saving on power bills, you will get excited and start trying out different ideas. There is no rule book. This book is a guide to give you ideas, get you started on the right track, and show you that anyone can do it. If a young, independent girl like myself can do it (purchase a house and pay it off) in seven years on a single income and still have a life and not go without, it is possible for anyone.

Finance and Loans

Some people frown upon getting financing for household items. But having something now and being able to pay it off a bit at a time can be used to your advantage. You work out what you require to pay back over the period, as long as you pay it off in the time period so you won't incur any fees.

CHAPTER SIX

THE FUN STUFF

Shopping

A girl's best friend ... shoes, well for most girls. Find your favourite stores and ask around if they offer membership discounts for signing up, especially if you're planning on a purchase. Why not get all the bells and whistles for the same price, if you can.

When shopping for electrical goods, coming from an ex-retailer (I use to work in an electrical store for five years of my career, I wanted to understand products available on the market and value for money), know what you're looking for first. There's no point in buying that TV with internet access when you don't even have Wi-Fi in the house. By the time you pay for the line rental and W-Fi on top of that, you need to ask yourself if this something you're actually going to use. Or is this just going to sit there for show and tell and gather dust? Quality does make a difference in how long a product lasts, and a warranty can save you in the long run from forking out hundreds of dollars to fix the item or replace it with another.

Nothing is worse than impulse buying, that is, buying because you think it's a good deal, only to get it home and realise you should've paid that little bit more for what you really wanted. Be aware of the impact of the lights, the shiny products in the showroom and the salesperson who comes across pushy and makes you feel obliged to purchase the product to get them to leave you alone. Or you can feel unsure but you go ahead and make the purchase because the salesperson seemed so sure of the product themselves or it's only on sale for a limited time with limited stock available.

Before buying high-priced electrical items, look up online what they're worth and how much you would expect to pay. That way you're going in armed with the knowledge and information to get the best value for the money and you purchase the item to your specific needs. When you do go in the store to purchase your product, make them aware that you have done your research and know what the product is worth. They want to have and keep your business. Don't keep them in the dark, playing price guessing. Tell them how much you're willing to pay and see what kind of a deal they can do for you.

Shopping for electrical items can be a big cost if you don't know what you're looking for. For example if you're looking at buying a new television, what size are you looking at? What features do you want? Would you use those features? There is no point in getting a television with Skype and internet when you don't know anyone with Skype to talk to. It's all about value for money. Once you have an idea in your mind of what you're looking for, check the product online to get an idea for value and cost of the product. Then you can start checking out major competitors, what bonuses they're throwing in or offering, and extra warranties.

There's no point in getting a free stereo when you don't need one, unless you're going to sell it and make yourself some money or use it as a gift to a family member for an upcoming birthday present. You can't bargain with someone if you don't know the value of the product you're purchasing. As they say, if you don't ask, you don't get. Just because the product is right for one person, doesn't mean that the product's right for you. Hence, why there are so many products available on the market?

There's such a broad market to cater to. Ring around and ask salespeople—that's what they're there for. Do your research and then you know what you're getting and whether you're getting the best deal that you're happy with. Don't take no for an answer. If it's realistic you can have it! My first dream car was my Ford Falcon Sedan (I see the head shakes and hear the disgruntled noises at me mentioning let alone admitting that I once drove a Ford). I had in mind what size, mileage and price range I wanted, but no particular brand. Car dealer after car dealer told me I had no chance of getting what I wanted. They pretty much laughed in my face. But I had a goal in mind. I had done my research and I wasn't giving in. Miss determination, I definitely can be at times.

Determination definitely paid off this time when I finally found it! I got what I wanted in the end. Don't give up! You can do it! That car was my pride and joy for five years. It did me well. Don't let anyone tell you no! If it's realistic and believable to you, you can strive towards it and achieve that goal your little heart desires.

Travel

Holidays are an important part of recovering and re-centring yourself, having a break and getting yourself ready for the next stage of your life. Traveling is very popular, as there is so much of this big wide world out there to experience and visit or a simple escape/get-away from your everyday surroundings and take in the culture and architecture it has to offer. Break free from the mundane routine of life and working.

You don't necessarily have to go overseas to enjoy yourself or stay in the fanciest hotel, although it is always definitely a pleasurable experience in itself. Good old camping and chilling in the quiet of the country can be just as fulfilling for some families and friends.

These days families and friends are scattered to all four corners of the world and around the country. There are always weddings, engagements, and birthday celebrations to share in, but even just staying in touch with family and friends can be the perfect excuse for a getaway. Plus if they're nice enough, they may even offer you a free bed or a couch to stay on for a night or more, if you're lucky.

Look at the cost of flights and accommodations. These will give you ideas of what is available and the cost, giving you a guide of how much to budget for. Set up a direct debit. As soon as your pay goes into your bank account, have an automatic direct debit set up to transfer money across to another account that you don't have access to. Remove the temptation of touching the money that's been put aside in that account. You don't want to set your savings too high that you sneak in and withdraw because you have no money to live with to buy everyday necessities.

Accommodation places can do bundles for extra nights that cost less than short stays. The off-peak season may bulge your suitcase with winter clothes but save you a lot of money and avoid all the screaming kids during school holidays. Everyone wants your business, so don't be rude. Tell them what deals you've come across and see if they can beat it. They might even surprise you and match it.

There's plenty of sightseeing and touristy things you can partake in without forking out a heap of money. Look into what you're interested in prior to travelling. Ask friends who have previously travelled there what they recommend or enjoyed doing. Even TripAdvisor.com has recommendations on the most popular activities at a destination.

Airline companies offer deals for flying at later times in the evening, when they don't get as much business. Some even price match other advertised fares.

Saving for Holidays

We all love a good holiday, a change of scenery, that feeling of escaping the mundane work, home life cycle. What better way to achieve this than by visiting inspired locations you've seen on friends social media accountants or those pesky advertisements' that pop up on your newsfeed reminding you how long it's been since you've had a break. Or they just so happen to be advertising that special place you've been thinking about visiting and offering a hard to resist deal. You don't necessarily have to go overseas or stay in the flashiest hotels. These days it's quite common that family and friends are scattered all around the country and the world. A good way to stay in touch is to go for a visit, plus they usually know the best places to go and things to do that only the locals know. You never know, you might get lucky and find yourself with a free bed or even a couch for the night to sleep on.

There are plenty of sightseeing and touristy things that you will want to take the opportunity to experience and make the most of your visit, as who knows when you'll be back there again. Look up on the internet what interests you and what you want to experience while you're there visiting. Ask friends who have travelled there before if they have any recommendations. There are always information brochures or magazines with information of what's available, the hot spots to go see, and the most popular things to experience.

Why not go check out the local art galleries, museums, or nature walks? They are usually free to go visit and explore or may charge a small fee like a gold coin donation to help maintain them. Experience the culture of the place you're visiting and indulge in the history and the culture that it has to offer. All towns and cities are so very different from the next and have something different to offer and experience.

There are many travel companies that offer travel packages including accommodation, meals and tours. Check what's available or ask a travel agent what deal they can do for you and you may be surprised what value for money you can receive. Even travelling off-peak times or midnight flights may be an option for you. Thus, you can save some money on flying to put towards something else that's more important or suits your needs and wants.

After you have saved money for your holidays, you need to figure out how far it will go. The best way is to work out how many days your trip is and divide up per day to give you a rough estimate of your daily spending allowance. For example, when I went to Bali I saved up $1,000 for eight days; therefore, I had approximately $100 to spend a day. The last day I still had money left over so I could splurge on buying gifts for friends or souvenirs to remember the trip, or I could keep the money towards my next visit. Obviously for other destinations you may need more than that depending on whether you're on a trip that includes meals or included extras like tours or the exchange rate at that particular time you're visiting. A good guide is to check the currency exchange rate so you know what your money is worth compared to theirs, giving you a rough idea on how much you will be paying for things.

It doesn't just come down to saving for the trip itself. Don't forget the tourist attractions you want to experience while you're over there. Who knows when you will visit that destination again, so experience the culture and all it has to offer. As they always say on my tours, if you really want to buy it, buy it. It's not like you have the opportunity to pop down the following week and go find that special artifact or souvenir again.

Packing is essential when overseas travelling. What we take for granted isn't necessarily as readily available where you're travelling to or come in the same form as you're used to buying. Some hotels provide mini-samples of toiletry basics that are enough to get you by. It's normal to live out of a suitcase and reuse clothes or handwash underwear while travelling. That was the way I was doing my washing the week I was staying in London. You do whatever you can to help you get by. If you have half-used products at home that you need to use up or you're only travelling for a small period of time, take the opportunity of using up what you've already got, while saving packaging and luggage weight at the same time.

If you're still saving up money for that big trip, that doesn't mean you can't get inspired and start planning where you want to go. That's all part of the fun. Visit travel agents for brochures or look up travel destinations online. Why not make a scrapbook highlighting all the amazing places you're going to experience and visit? That way when you do have the time off from work and the money saved up you'll know exactly what you want, where you want to go and what adventures you want to experience and immerse yourself in.

If going overseas is too much or too far away for the time off that you have available, why not experience your own backyard? Become a tourist in your own neck of the woods. That way when you've visitors, you can show them how amazing it is where you live. There are always travel guides and tourist information offices offering things to go do that you probably wouldn't even have thought of adventuring to or experiencing.

The Fun Stuff

Like many of you, I like going to the movies and going out for dinner with friends, but when you do it all the time it does start to add up. Don't get me wrong, you can still go out and enjoy yourself. Some restaurants give you discounts for your loyalty.

Fitness

You don't have to spend a lot of money at a gym to keep fit. There is nothing worse than paying fortnightly for a gym membership and not actually going and getting the benefits of where your money is going. Some gyms allow you to pay as you go for classes. You can even get free apps for your phone with yoga or target-toning workouts.

Workout DVDs watched at home are a cheap way to avoid the wet weather in the winter or streaming online via YouTube. Mind you, I don't mind the refreshing feel of the raindrops splashing on your face as you dodge the puddles and listen to the crunch of your raincoat as your arms swish back and forth. Another idea is to get a group of friends to exercise together. This keeps each other motivated as you don't want to let the other down if they're reliant on you to meet up for a morning session catch-up. Look up workouts online to create your own plan or circuit. You don't need expensive equipment to stay fit and motivated.

I always try to stay fit and healthy. That's not to say that I don't give in and overindulge in yummy treats that I shouldn't be eating, but life is all about balance in all areas of life. My excuse for why I go to the gym is so I can eat. There are so many things that you can do even if you don't have a gym membership. The problem a lot of people have is that they fork all this money out for a membership and then they don't go, or something else comes up. There are so many other things that you could be spending your money on. I even went to the extreme of running around the backyard because I was too embarrassed to run around the local park due to the neighbours coming out to watch me run by.

Walking really is just as good as any other fitness workout. See what works for you. You don't have to punish yourself just to see results. Persistence is the key. If health is your priority though, sometimes you can't put a price on it and you'd be happy to go without your morning caffeine fix to fit in a class motivational session. What are your priorities? They don't have to be the same as everyone else's and they shouldn't be. This is your journey—your life experience. If something isn't making you happy, only you can change that and make something else work for you and to your advantage.

You don't have to be the next Olympian to work out or be booked into the next marathon, though that may be a future goal for you to work towards. Give yourself that initial push in the beginning by remembering what you're working towards. If you don't feel inspired you can always invite a friend along, or go to a local walking track by the beach where everybody's out and about walking their dogs or going for a run. Inspiration comes from being surrounded by other fitness-inclined people, who give you that extra push of motivation. What I like to do is go for a walk to a friend's place for a visit. That way I'm getting my fitness in at the same time as a social call.

There are hundreds of fitness DVDs available out there, which you can watch in the comfort of your own home at whatever time is convenient to you until you feel comfortable going to a gym. I'm also a fan of is buying some indoor equipment like steppers for really cheap prices, and they work wonders on your butt.

One thing I've been taking advantage of is free gym trials. I really enjoy the classes, because you don't have to think of what to do next and they push you along when you're lacking motivation or exhausted towards the end and need to push through to the end. The vibe in those classes, with the excited chatter prior to commencing, the loud dance music and everyone there for the same reason—to keep fit—leaves you on a high for the rest of your day.

CHAPTER SEVEN

THE WAY TO HAVE EVERYTHING WITHOUT SACRIFICES

If something is really important to you and you don't want to go without or sacrifice it, then don't. If you do, you will only want to spend more money than you were probably originally going to spend anyway. What's important to you may not be as important to someone else and that's fine. You don't need to compare yourself to anyone else. We're all here on our own journey with our own goals and dreams that we have passion and drive towards. Use that motivation and that inspiration, as you'll never know where it might just lead you.

I am one of those girls who has tried the whole compromise thing, and yes, I still want the best. You can have the best. It's all about balancing priorities, your goals and what you want to achieve. I'm talking from even the simple things, from toiletries to clothes. Especially in today's society, there are so many stores available to purchase from and online too.

It is nice to go to beauty salons and get spoilt every now and then. But you need to weigh up the cost: is it cost efficient to you or is it an every-now-and-then treat for yourself. Online stores and pharmacies sell nail kits (from gel to shellac) and treatment masks a lot cheaper than the cost of going into the salon and getting the treatment done. Why not invite friends around for a social evening while cleansing and having a catch up at the same time? It's also a sense of achievement when people ask you where you got your nails done and tell them you did it yourself, while saving money at the same time.

Okay, so I love reading my magazines, even back as a teenager chilling at a friend's house reading the Dolly Doctor in *Dolly Magazine*. Research how much it costs to purchase your magazine every month off the shelf of a retail store. Would a year's subscription be cheaper? I wait until a magazine advertises an awesome freebie with a subscription as an incentive for you to commit to purchasing the magazine for the coming year. It's often something that I was going to buy at the shops or something that's normally too expensive to splash out on. I've received everything from a hair-treatment pack or a tanning kit to a make-up goodie bag including eyeliner, moisturiser and mascara. Today, my excitement came with a knock at the door with a beauty gift pack courtesy of my most recent yearly magazine subscription.

If you're the kind of girl who sees the latest glossy magazine and you have to buy it, look at the subscriptions they have on offer. I wait until a freebie I really want comes up, like a combined magazine package or body-treatment pack. There's no point in getting something for free and never using it.

You still need to have the fun stuff and special treats to make saving and budgeting that more worthwhile with incentives. Publishers also do deals every now and then that combine multiple magazines for a small fee. Some libraries also carry current issues you can borrow for free.

There are always plenty of vouchers or deals and discount offers for first-time customers or if purchasing in bulk. Organise with your work colleagues or friends to go halves in the product if it's something you are both interested in purchasing, which will bring the cost down. Even becoming a member at your favourite store can usually bring you bulk deals and discounts for your return business.

Once friends understand that you don't have a lot of money to spend, then they are more inclined to offer and suggest options that are available or things that they have tried. You never know—they may be in exactly the same position as you. They might want to spend less money but haven't had the courage to speak up about it and would quite happily partake in your money-saving methods.

CHAPTER EIGHT

THINK OUTSIDE THE BOX

Surprisingly, there are things you can save money on that you wouldn't even think you would be able to make a saving on. My front window used to get a lot of light in and heat up the front of the house, thus costing a fair bit of money to run an air conditioner or warm that room up during winter when the windows frosted up. I spoke to a friend and got my window tinted for a good price, which definitely made a difference with the changing seasons. I didn't even know this friend was even in the business of tinting windows. Mates usually give you a good price in hope that you'll recommend them to someone else at the same time helping them to generate new business. These days the saying "it's not what you know, but who you know" definitely holds its weight in gold.

I know that some people aren't a fan of public transport, but let us look at its advantages. I grew up catching trains because they were close and convenient to where I lived and the fact that it's a cheaper alternative to using your own vehicle, saves clocking up mileage on your vehicle and saves forking out extra money on fuel. You don't have to worry about finding a place to park or paying for parking.

Incidentally, you can meet some nice people on the train too. You can watch the scenery pass by outside the window, and it's a perfect time to zone out and meditate from everything that's going on in your life. Relax and take a book to read with you, and the time and trip will be over and done with and you'll be at your destination before you know it. Catching public transport is a perfect way to have a big night out without having to organise a designated driver or paying for an overpriced taxi that's going the long route to your destination.

Riding the train is a perfect way to get you out of your comfort zone and prepares you for travelling in other countries when you're left with no other option of how to get around. You wouldn't want to miss out on seeing the sights or going out for a group dinner due to misconceptions on travelling via public transport.

Make Money on the Side

Tax time is something that you should be planning and organising from the beginning of the new financial year. As you purchase uniforms and or other work items, keep the receipts in a special spot like an envelope and keep a tally as you go. That way at tax time you're not looking for receipts or missing out on claiming back money you're entitled to. If you're not 100% about what you're entitled to claim, I would recommend a tax agent. Sure there is a fee, which you can claim the following year at tax time, but they will make you aware of a lot of things that you can claim that you may not be aware of and make it a stress-free time for you.

Using Your Skills

Are there things that you are good at or have a natural flair for? Do you have a creative activity that you enjoy doing? Are you good at arts and crafts? You could always set up a stall at the market selling freshly baked cookies, vegetables from your garden or candles. Even children still do car washes or lemonade stands to make some spare change to help out around the house.

Things That You No Longer Use

If you need to declutter and make a few dollars at the same time, have a garage sale. You paid good money for those items and you no longer use them, but someone else always wants a bargain these days. There are many selling options, such as gumtree (online classified advertisements), eBay and newspapers, but if you want to get rid of everything in one big hit all at once, have a nice big clean out and start fresh.

Make sure you advertise well and price items clearly. There's no point going to all this effort of planning and organising only to have no one show up. Word of mouth through friends only reaches so many people. Branch out to hit your target audience, those people who are looking for a deal and a bargain. You may have other items they're looking for. If you're not using them you may as well get something for them and give them to someone who will use and appreciate them. Those extra dollars can be put towards a bill, saved for a holiday, or used to spoil yourself for a night out, something you don't normally get to indulge in. That extra money makes life that little bit easier to get by.

We all have our favourite boots or handbags that get worn to death and then find it's been replaced by a newer model not quite like the one that you previously had and loved. Get your handbags and boots to last longer by spending that little extra time and money on a protective spray to extend their lifespan, protecting them in different weather conditions.

If you're like me there will come a time when you'll suddenly realise you've got all this stuff that you no longer use or have a need for. Examples include excess gym equipment, DVD players and portable convenience electrical goods. Your unwanted goods are another person's treasure. I've found some local stores like pawn shops that are willing to take in your goods for a small price if you can't gather enough items for a garage sale. Alternatively there's always your friends. You could get all your unwanted items together and hold a combined garage sale if you don't have enough items to hold one on your own.

Books are a big part of my life, and I even reread them. If I don't like them or didn't enjoy them, then I sell them after I've read them. If you don't get offers after trying to sell online on various marketplaces, you can donate them to charity, at least it's not extra waste and you're donating to charity at the same time. Quite a few bookstores and markets offer a book exchange. If you know you're never going to read the book again, why not exchange it for something you've been eyeing or start a new series?

I found as I grow older that I seem to be reading less. Having a quiet moment to oneself and unwinding just doesn't seem as important as the everyday mundane tasks that we find so much more important than having some "me time." Put yourself first, and make some time for yourself—fill yourself up first.

Once you get back into the joy of escaping to another world, the imagination and relaxation will transport you to another place. What did you enjoy reading as a child? Are there any actors that you follow or are interested in their journey that inspire you? Do you enjoy gardening guides or scrapbooking ideas? The list is endless. There are clubs that you can join to order books from or start a book swap club with friends or online.

Gift Ideas

When it comes to gift ideas it really is the thought that counts. These days most people already own everything. Rather than wait for things, we just go out and get them. Today's society is the society that wants everything yesterday, if they don't already have it. Set a limit of how much you're willing to spend and make sure you stick to it, just like your food shopping list. There's no point spending money on items that you already own or have absolutely no use for.

Vouchers (known as gift cards or credit cards you load a certain amount of money onto which are valid at any store) are quite popular and acceptable as gifts these days, especially when family and friends are far and wide around the country or world. The fees for sending a parcel can outweigh the cost of the gift sometimes if you're not careful what items you choose to send. Plus these days people usually buy what they want when they want it, so there's no point buying a gift that they've already got or are not going to use.

Why not do something a bit more personal or memorable? Get creative and design a calendar or a scrapbook from your year of special moments. Design a coffee mug with a favourite photo or quote, something that the family will see and use every day. Buy someone a magazine subscription, and they will think of you every time the magazine arrives in their letterbox.

When it comes to Christmas cards and gift wrap, you don't need to spend a lot of money to get something nice with meaning. The cheap dollar stores and buy in bulk discount stores are perfect for picking up bulk Christmas cards and gift wrap. The number of family birthday cards that you need to purchase over the year can add up. Why pay $6 for something that most people just throw in the bin when you can buy just as nice or hilarious cards for a third of the price? Little things like this all add up and make a difference. How many engagement parties do you attend? How many friends hold baby showers? It all adds up, and it is definitely the small things that add up to make the difference. As a kid we always made cards for mother's day and father's day—it's thoughtful and creative.

These days people usually buy everything they want when they want it or when they see it. A really thoughtful gift idea is a scrapbook or photo album, memories of your friends or family, something that they can cherish forever. It brings back memories while you're creating the scrapbook too.

Over the Christmas period, instead of sending Christmas cards I hand deliver them to save on postage fees. For those friends who are living in nearby suburbs, it's a perfect opportunity to pop around for a friendly catch up at the same time.

Hobbies

Everyone has hobbies they like or teams they support or follow. Collectables can be an expensive hobby to have, but I myself love scrapbooking. I may not be the fanciest, but there are so many inspiring ideas out there. You can print photos at home for yourself or for gifts. Otherwise these days photo shops do regular specials offering 10 cents for each photo printed.

CONCLUSION

POSITIVE REINFORCEMENT

Let friends know that you're trying to save money and suggest catch ups involving minimal spending of money. Invite them around to your place for a coffee. You get to talk to them in the comfort of your own home without having to rush around or hear the noise of other customers in a shop. You could always go for a walk together, as getting into fitness always has its benefits. It's more fun and feels less like working out when you're doing it with a friend. These days even the beaches have their own fitness equipment set up alongside the bike track, where you can stop and follow the exercise for each equipment on the signs. You don't need to spend thousands of dollars on gym memberships that don't fit into your schedule or that you're not getting the benefits from.

Remain Motivated

We as humans tend to take things for granted and appreciate things less after a while once their lustre has worn off. The longer that you're in a place whether it's the current home or city that you live in, the more it loses its excitement—it's like that with anything. The novelty wears off as it becomes familiar every day.

Your home may be exciting to someone who has never lived in that area, never seen those sights, nor experienced what you take for granted on a daily basis. We should see our homes and what we have with fresh eyes of appreciation. We need to learn to see things from a different light with new eyes. Learn to appreciate things for what they actually are.

Develop gratitude for what you have and then you don't have to spend money on things you truly don't need. It's about having life balance. We could be here for a short time or we could be here for a long time, no one knows. It's all about choosing what is your priority? Balance is the key. In light of that, there are always new and exciting things to experience in your area or within an hour's drive in another direction. Use that as a cheap getaway or holiday to experience in your area until you get your fix or that big trip you've been planning all year. Go to a travel agent for a brochure about destinations that you're interested in travelling to. Find out what deals are available. That way when you do have the money available, you won't be rushing into anything and will have already done the exciting part, your research.

It's the in-thing to save a few dollars. People get excited about what deals they were able to receive and want to share and pass on their ideas and experiences. Join in!

www.ingramcontent.com/pod-product-compliance
Lightning Source LLC
LaVergne TN
LVHW011858060526
838200LV00054B/4404